MY PHENOMENAL
TIBET JOURNEY

TENZIN CHOEKYI

AuthorHouse™ UK
1663 Liberty Drive
Bloomington, IN 47403 USA
www.authorhouse.co.uk
Phone: 0800.197.4150

Published by AuthorHouse 12/21/2018

ISBN: 978-1-7283-8272-2 (sc)
ISBN: 978-1-7283-8271-5 (e)

Print information available on the last page.

Any people depicted in stock imagery provided by Getty Images are models, and such images are being used for illustrative purposes only. Certain stock imagery © *Getty Images.*

This book is printed on acid-free paper.

Because of the dynamic nature of the Internet, any web addresses or links contained in this book may have changed since publication and may no longer be valid. The views expressed in this work are solely those of the author and do not necessarily reflect the views of the publisher, and the publisher hereby disclaims any responsibility for them.

authorHOUSE®

I wish to thank my Mom and Dad for their support on publishing my first book.

Special thanks to Mrs. Ringmo and Ms. Moughton for helping us with the editing.

Dear readers,

My name is Choekyi, I am six years old. I am living in London.

This is my first time writing a book. The title of the book is (My Phenomenal Tibet Journey). I would like to share my book with you because it is different from where I am living now.

When I write long words it's really hard to spell them all correctly. It takes a long time to do all the writing. Sometimes, it is confusing, but you never give up and you will never know unless you try.

It is easy to get ideas because I went to Tibet and I have pictures in front of me. I am glad that I have a dictionary so I use it for different adjectives instead of using the same describing words.

Yours sincerely,

Tenzin Choekyi

Table of Contents

About Tibet

There are three amazing regions in Tibet: U-Tsang, Kham and Amdo. The ancient city of Tibet is located in the continent of Asia.

The pretty Spring season is like a colourful garden full of flowers.

During the Summer, the warm summer sun often shines brightly in the light blue sky.

In the chilly Autumn, it feels like the world has turned golden!

The cold Winter brings snow and the whole place changes to a snowy part of the world.

Preparation

Before you go to Tibet, you need to have these things in your luggage:

First Aid Kit

Visa

Clothes

Luggage

Camera

Passport

- A passport is used so everyone knows who you are and you also need to apply for a visa. A visa is used to give you permission from the Chinese embassy to let you enter the country. When the special people say: "Yes, you can come to our country," you are then allowed to go. When you get to the airport, you need to show them your passport and visa.
- A first aid kit is useful when you get hurt or someone falls over on the way.
- Clothes in Tibet are special and pretty but you still need to take some clothes with you.
- A camera is the most important thing to take. If you don't have a camera, then no one can take beautiful pictures of the amazing places.

The Way People are Welcomed

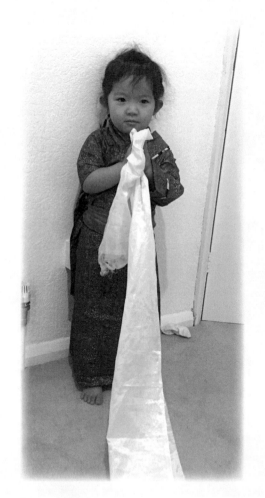

Tibetan people give long shining Khada to guests or visitors and wonderful family from different countries. A long white Khada is made from soft fluffy silk. They symbolise the pure heart of the giver.

I was very impressed because my fantastic family gave me lots of white long Khada. The wonderful people there give white shining Khada when their relatives arrive from a different country.

When I arrived in the crowded airport, all of my relatives put Khada around my neck to welcome me and my family.

Tibetan Food

Tibetan people normally eat delicious and scrumptious food called Tsamba. This is roasted barley made from yellow and white wheat powder.

Tibetan people use Choo to make Tsamba powder. They put a small amount of roasted barley into the hole of Choo and they string it round and round many times to make Tampa.

First, you need put a little hot boiling water in the bowl. Next, you put small piece of yellow yak butter in the bowl. After that you put in wheat powder and dried yellow cheese and sugar.

Then, you mix all the ingredients together to make Tsamba dough.

Finally, you eat the mouth-watering, light brown Tsamba dough. The brown Tsamba tastes sweet and it makes you no longer feel hungry. The Tsamba tastes amazing and lovely and the wheat powder tastes nice.

I like the wheat powder because it's as white as the clouds and fluffy. It makes me happy and the flavour amazes me.

The yellow butter and cheese comes from female Yak.

The nomad people milk the female yak and put the milk in the wooden bucket. You need to shake it up and down many times without stopping.

After a while, the butter separates from the skim milk. Then the skim milk is boiled and turns into small pieces of cheese which they let dry in the hot sun.

The cheeses are hard because they get dried from the heat of the sun.

About the Clothes

There are so many different types of traditional clothes in Tibet. The ladies wear amazing jewels.

Women's clothes are full-length and men are shorter.

The top of the Tibetan clothes is thinner than English clothes and the dress is made of a much thicker material. Some people wear traditional Tibetan clothes when they have celebrations.

The astonishing jewels are as colourful as the rainbow. If you saw the jewels you would be shocked. The edge of dress is decorated with incredibly beautiful stitching.

The dress is multi-coloured. The red long belt is tied around your waist. It helps you to keep the dress on properly.

The Nomad Hairstyle

Some nomad hairstyles are beautiful and unique. This style made me feel magical!

The nomad hairstyle is worn for celebrations and parties. The nomad hairstyle takes more than an hour to create, so you need to be patient.

The Tibetan Tent

The Tibetan tent is traditionally made from Yak's wool. Normally, Tibetan nomad people live in tents. When I visited this huge tent, I felt like I was in a dream. There were so many things in tent like pans, wooden spoons and the kitchen is huge. It was so interesting.

Tibetan Tashi Dhargey: 8 symbols which are painted on white fabric tent. "*The 8 symbols are Conch, Umbrella, Banner, Fish, Wheel, Knot, Lotus. These seven emblems merge into one from the shape of vase.*" This tent is used for people to have birthday parties and celebrations inside.

About the Religion

Religion is very important for Buddhists. Some temples are painted in gold and have wall paintings and Buddha statues inside. The temples

are important because they have been in Tibet for a very long time.

The colourful prayer wheels surrounds the outside of the temple. When you are going round the temple it means that you are praying.

I was so excited to see the colourful prayer wheels, which I want to see again.

The huge monastery is called Lanrun Gar.
This monastery is home for 40,000 monks, nuns and lay students.

They study not only the religion, they also study arts and so many other things.

This is a huge prayer wheel spinning by the nice clean water.

The sands paint

This is the most beautiful sands paint in the whole wide world and it's called Mandala. First, you need to dye the sand, after you use the Chak-pur to paint it.

Chak-pur is a tool used for Tibetan sand painting. I hope that I can paint a Mandala in the future.

Lungta flags

Lungta flags have 5 colours: they are blue, white, yellow, green and red. Tibetan people normally hang the flag on top of the mountains.

Tibetan people usually hang them on one pole, somewhere in a higher place. It brings you good luck.

Tibetan animals

By the Tso Ngonpo there were yaks, sheep, horses and there were some camels for people to ride. This was my most favourite part of my journey.

Tso Ngonpo is the largest lake I have ever seen in my life.

I really had fun riding on the yaks, horses and camels. All these things were so amazing to me.

I tried to touch a baby yak, but it ran away from me! Yaks are very special, only Tibetan people have them. You can't find them anywhere else in the world. Tibetan nomads cannot live without yaks.